AF265467

Published in 2018 by Susan Haynes-Elcock in Great Britain

Copyright © Susan Haynes-Elcock 2018

The moral right of the author has been asserted
ISBN 978-0-9570040-5-4

A copy of the CIP data is available from the British Library on request.

Foreword by Father 'DD' Haynes

Edited by Tony Kelly

Printed in UK

Layout and design by mgdesignbds

Written by Susan Haynes-Elcock

This Susan Haynes-Elcock gift book is a thoughtful,
empowering and impactful gift. If it inspires you – spread the word;
tell others, recommend or gift it to your favourite person.

Random Thoughts

...for Your Journey

Susan
HAYNES-ELCOCK

A SUSAN HAYNES-ELCOCK GIFTBOOK

Foreward

There is an immediacy, a 'suddenly' about the writings contained in **Random Thoughts.**

The author, my dearest sibling, Susan Haynes-Elcock has captured the truth of an ancient adage which annunciates – "the journey of a thousand miles begins with a single step" (Lao Tzu).

Indeed she heralds the fact that within the darkness of our life's journey – 'Random Thoughts' can break through as a bright ray of light, showing the way with its transcendence of power, faith, hope and the summoning of our will to survive.

Within each page of the short bursts of thought I have discovered, once again, how insightful, impacting and exhilarating words can be. I pray that you will find the wisdom, hope and that sudden breakthrough for your tomorrow.

Fr. Don 'DD' Haynes
Anglican Priest/Counsellor/Educator
St Bartholomew by The Sea
The Berry Islands
The Bahamas

"…Therefore be at peace with God,
Whatever you conceive Him to be…"

Desiderata
Max Ehrmann

Inspirational, motivational
down to earth and empowering
random thoughts
to help you on your journey

Everyone's journey is different though some of the
challenges we face may be similar.
Our circumstance determines our journey.
Our journeys are a time of trial and triumph.
During our journeys we need much self-reliance,
support and courage to find our peaceful place.
We can grow and develop positively to become the best
human being we can be.

I hope **RANDOM THOUGHTS ...for your journey**
will be of help to you on your journey to your positive place.

Dedicated to my beautiful Mother, Mumah Genie
who took another step in her journey
on Tuesday, 29 November 2016.

It's often tough to get to the next step

Just take a leap of faith

 believe through the good times

the in-between times and the bad

that you will be...and that you are...

"The Lord is my Shepherd

I shall not want...."

23 Psalm: 1-2

It's 12:00 midnight

The only sound to be heard

is the passing of the trains.

As I look through my window

and breathe in the rain-fresh scent

of the night I am filled

with hope for a better journey

for the NEW YEAR.

My first grand-child

Is here to start his journey

I am filled with

such love for him

He makes me believe that
"Children are a heritage from
the LORD
offspring a reward from him"

Psalm 127: 3

"Love will save the day."

Whitney Houston

Hebrews 13

"For he hath said, I will never leave thee
nor forsake thee."

Remember that
though family and friends
may forsake
Your Spiritual Advisor is always there
...the footprints in your sand.

Footprints In The Sand

Anonymous

"…Lord, you said once I decided to follow you,
You'd walk with me all the way.
But I noticed that during the saddest
and most troublesome times of my life,
there was only one set of footprints.
I don't understand why,
when I needed You the most,
You would leave me."

He whispered, "My precious child,
I love you and will
never leave you
Never, ever
During your trials and testings.
When you saw only one set of footprints,
it was then I carried you…"

Your journey begins from that

first planted seed

to living all cosy warm in the womb

coming out hollering and shouting into the world

missing that warmth and free meals

growing up doing all the baby things

until that first step

your beginning bid for freedom

and independence

Your little baby steps become

sometimes giant ones

Such is your journey

it's called life

your life

your hopes

your dreams

your good times, bad times, sad times, happy
times

All yours to mould and shape

using the strength and faith that's **YOU**

I hope you are there

Because

TODAY

I need your strength

wisdom

and understanding

to guide me

through the

treacherous paths

of my journey

As I prayed for strength and grace
I came across this.

2 Timothy 3:1-8
English Standard Version (ESV)

Godlessness in the Last Days

"But understand this.
That in the last days
there will come times of difficulty.
For people will be lovers of self,
lovers of money,
proud, arrogant, abusive,
disobedient to their parents,
ungrateful, unholy, heartless,
unappeasable, slanderous,
without self-control,
brutal, not loving good,
treacherous, reckless,
swollen with conceit,
lovers of pleasure rather
than lovers of God,
having the appearance
of godliness,
but denying its power.
avoid such people...corrupted in mind
and disqualified regarding the faith. "

"...Take kindly

the counsel of the years

gracefully surrendering

the things of youth..."

Desiderata
Max Ehrmann

Our life's journey

Will take us through

many valleys and peaks.

It will never be

as we envisioned

But know this,

it will be what it is

Spring clean it like you

would your house

Understand that a GPS

won't help you on this journey

Bad things and trouble

are nought

but lessons

on your journey

Learn them well.

life is hope

life is faith

life is peace,

life is confidence

life is friendship

life is memories

life is courage

life cannot invade soul

life is eternal life

life is love

You champion me

In the simplest

of ways

And for that

I am thankful

Friday, 22 September 2017

Today I met someone who
has been diagnosed with cancer
the prognosis is not good
yet she is so positive
she empowers
and motivates me
by her strength
and her faith
her laughter and
her positive outlook

Through the sadness,

disappointments

tragedies and fire of pain

we rise like the Phoenix

from the ashes

You will find your place of

understanding when you

least expect it.

Since my Mumah Genie died
Every day I pray
That the pain would become
A little easier to bear
It never goes away
completely
but day by day
it becomes
more manageable
as I remember the good times
the bad times
the fun times
the naughty jokes times
and what a wonderful human
being
and role model she was
for me and many others

Faith helps us conquer

the demons in us

"Success is failure turned inside out –"

Author Unknown

From the Poem Don't Quit

"…Life is queer with its twists and turns,

As every one of us sometimes learns,

And many a failure turns about,

When he might have won if he'd stuck it out.

Don't give up, though the pace seems slow –

You may succeed with another blow…"

Author unknown

IF

by Rudyard Kipling

"...IF you can keep your head
when all about you
are losing theirs
and blaming it on you...
and everything that's in it,
And - which is more -
you'll be a Man, my son..."

"If at first you don't succeed

Try and try again

Never give up

Death is only another stage

in your journey

Make your life matter

find that peace

within yourself.

Ask

"what will I leave behind?"

"what will be my legacy?"

Family is the

most important

thing in your life

Honour, care and cherish it

as even though

you each have

your own journey

your paths are

always intertwined.

If it's one thing that
holds true is that
thoughts tossed
into the universe
make a difference
to the world's
spiritual well-being.

I read somewhere recently

that no matter what it is

if the Lord intended

for it to happen

It will.

This might not be

the life you planned

It's the only one you have

Live it

Love it

Embrace it

With light, joy and laughter

*"It is during your
darkest moments that
you must focus to see the light."*

Aristotle

Success comes with

new hopes,

new thought

new dreams,

new strengths

And a new you

Believe that

you can.....

Whoever said 'put away childish things'

Never played snow angels

Ate ice cream in the snow

Jumped and splashed in rain puddles

Crunched autumn leaves underfoot

Stuck their tongue out at a stranger

Release the child in you.

Roller blade

Jump rope

Rap as if your life depends on it

Dance as if each day was your last

Cause age don't matter

It was a dream
I'll always remember
because my mum
was your messenger.
now I can slowly
but surely move on
with my journey
to rebuild my life
cause she told me
I would be alright

The joy

of giving back

of sharing

of caring

of smiling

of saying hello to a stranger

of loving unconditionally

cannot

be

described

in words

Open the curtains

of doubt

let the sun in

be your own future.

create your own hope.

whatever your beliefs,

honour your creator

as a child

of the universe

Footprints In The Sand
(song)

"And just when

I thought I'd lost my way

You gave me strength

to carry on

That's when I heard you say

I promise you

I'm always there

when your heart

is filled with sorrow

and despair

and I'll carry you

when you need a friend

you'll find my

footprints

in the sand"

British singer, Leona Lewis

Open your heart
to those
less fortunate
smile and then
smile some more
live as if today
was your last.

"just be true
to yourself and others"

Always believe that you can
And that you are worthy

It's your life
How do you want
it to look?
Who do you want
on your journey?
Are they on
the same page?
Do they have
your back?
Have you found
your peaceful space?

"Love will save the day"

Whitney Houston

Give yourself a

hug every day

Soothe your spirit,

soul and mind

Massage your

well being

A little smile goes a long long way

"Whatever you do
Do it heartily as to the Lord
And not to men
Knowing that from the Lord
You will receive
The reward of the inheritance
Or you serve the Lord Jesus"

Colossians 3:23-24

"It's hard to see the sunshine through
The rain but never give in"

Whitney Houston

Survival in this world

is about FAITH

Every day

is about FAITH

FAITH never loses

You even though

You might lose it

FAITH is the

jewel at the end

Of your journey

Beginning TODAY

Live your life

Live your Faith

don't let It

live you

New Year

New hopes

New dreams

New beginnings

New journeys

New motivations

New plans

New resolutions

New YOU

Soar above the clouds

have faith

AND

always remember

your heart is your canvas

paint the journey you want

"Tomorrow is always today!"

Susan Haynes-Elcock

Random Thoughts for Your Journey...is the second book in the motivational gift book series of Susan Haynes-Elcock.

With words of inspiration and motivational empowerment, it is meant to give hope and continued faith to you, my readers as you travel your life's journey

Susan says, "We all need to have faith, hope and spiritual well being to help us cope through our life's journey. Writing this book has kept me inspired with hope for the continuance of my exciting and challenging journey, and with the hope of giving you encouragement on yours."

Susan lives in London, UK. She has two grown children, Omari and Shanni and a grandson, Areli.

Susan is a supporter and volunteer of the charity, Refuge, which supports abused women and children **https://www.refuge.org.uk** as well as a supporter of Diabetes UK **www.diabetes.org.uk**

www.ingramcontent.com/pod-product-compliance
Lightning Source LLC
Chambersburg PA
CBHW061056050726
47592CB00004B/1703